Lucky Sods

A play

John Godber

Samuel French — London
New York - Toronto - Hollywood

LUCKY SODS

Lucky Sods was first performed by Hull Truck Theatre Company at Hull Truck Theatre on 9th April, 1995. It transferred to the Hampstead Theatre, London, on 20th September, 1995. The cast was as follows:

Morris	Iain Rogerson
Jean	Christine Cox
Norman	Nick Lane
Annie	Janet Dibley
Mother	Janet Dibley
Connie	Janet Dibley
Vicar	Nick Lane
Waiter	Nick Lane

Directed by John Godber
Designed by John Godber
Lighting by George Morris

ACT I

SCENE 1

A large raked stage. A standard lamp, two chairs and a TV with no back to it are the only pieces of furniture. House Lights, and preset fade to Black-out

Jean and Morris enter. Jean is in her early forties; she is sitting with her feet up, watching the box. Morris is a few years younger. Morris is standing away from the TV. Hot Chocolate's It Started with a Kiss *plays*

Lights come up quickly as music quickly fades. Jean and Morris have been watching "The National Lottery Live". They haven't won; as the Lights fade up they groan in unison at their disappointment at not winning

Jean Oh, I'll tell you this; what I wouldn't do if I won twenty million!
Morris Why, what wouldn't you do?
Jean Well, I wouldn't give you any of it for a start!
Morris Very good, a mile offside, but very good.
Jean Look at that, I didn't get a number…
Morris Neither did I.
Jean I usually get one at least.
Morris I'll never win it, I've had my share of good luck marrying you.
Jean I usually get one.
Morris Well, you're lucky then, aren't you?
Jean I've not been lucky this week, have I?
Morris You've got more chance of flying to the bloody moon than winning that.
Jean Twenty million this week. Somebody somewhere…

Morris drifts around the house and picks up a paper

Morris Forty-one in August and my life's just going.
Jean And mine isn't?

Morris Oh, I can't talk to you any more.

Jean No, answer me, Morris, do you think mine isn't?

Morris I'm not saying that.

Jean Because my life's going as well, in fact I sit in that chair sometimes and I wonder where the bloody hell the last twenty years have gone. That's why I do this, at least it gives me sommat to do.

Morris This is what I'm saying, we're both in the same boat. But I had something different and you've only just started work again.

Jean Seven years ago.

Morris It's not a competition.

Jean I've been at the video shop for seven years.

Morris All right, seven years.

Jean Seven years last March. And that's flown.

Morris They never get any decent videos in that bloody shop anyway, can't you do sommat about it?

Jean They do.

Morris I'll tell you something in the last seven years I bet you haven't seen a decent bloody film from that video shop.

Jean You wouldn't know a good one anyway!

Morris All I'm saying is, I miss the excitement.

Jean What, playing Goole Trades and Labour Club was exciting?

Morris It was.

Jean How?

Morris Well, you were lucky if you got out alive.

Jean But you were never at home.

Morris I'm never at home now, am I?

Jean It was every night though. Weekends. Every night.

Morris All I'm saying is, it was exciting, it was something different every night. And when I think of sitting in that hut watching over a scrap yard from ten till eight, for the next fifteen years. The thought of playing *Three Times a Lady* in New Biggin Social Club is very enticing!

Jean I know why you miss it.

Morris I've just told you why I miss it, Jean.

Jean Don't give me that.

Morris Why do I miss it then?

Jean Because of her.

Morris Who?

Jean You know who.

Morris Connie?

Jean Come on...

Morris What?

Jean You always fancied her.

Morris What?

Jean (*mocking him*) What? Don't come the innocent.

Morris Oh, come on.

Jean You fancied her right from the start.

Morris Oh eh...?

Jean Did you think I didn't know?

Morris Oh eh, come on?

Jean She knew you did and all.

Morris How did she?

Jean She played up to you.

Morris No, she...

Jean She knew.

Morris I didn't fancy her.

Jean You were too slow to make a move, you mean?

Morris I haven't seen her for three years.

Jean You knew who I meant though?

Morris That's funny that is.

Jean Yeh, but you knew who I meant.

Morris Jean?

Jean You knew who I meant.

Morris There was only one bloody woman in the band. Unless you thought I was having a fling with Gordon. Mind you to be honest I always thought Gordon fancied me.

Jean And you think you're funny.

Morris I'm not as funny as you.

Jean No, you're not.

Morris I know that. The sad thing is you don't know when you're being funny.

Jean All you do is shout.

Morris I'm not shouting now, am I?

Jean I'm glad you work most nights.

Morris So am I. I've been having nightmares this last month.

Jean I've never been able to get a good night's sleep with you anyway. You're all over the bed.

Morris Where has this come from?

Jean In fact, you make me wonder about you.

Morris I thought you were on about me shouting? Gooor you've got to
  have a brain like Einstein to keep up with you.
Jean You've always been all over the bed.
Morris Well, I'm not all over you.
Jean I know that.
Morris I'm not all over you.
Jean You never have been.
Morris Where has all this come from?
Jean You never have been really.
Morris I have.
Jean It's like sleeping with a barrel organ. You snore like an old pig.
Morris See what I mean. Jean, I can't keep up with you love.
Jean Your chins wobble when you snore.
Morris Oh right.
Jean Your stomach's all over the place.
Morris Oh right.
Jean It's like sleeping with somebody who's pregnant.
Morris We've mentioned Connie have we?
Jean And your breath…?
Morris This is why they have television. It's to stop people like us
  speaking to each other like this.
Jean You get on your back and you start snoring straight away.
  Sometimes I hold your nose. That stops you.
Morris There's no wonder, is there.
Jean I hold your nostrils together till you waken up.
Morris You don't, do you?
Jean I just pinch your nostrils together that stops you.
Morris There's no wonder I'm having nightmares, is there, I'm sleeping
  with Dr Crippen!

Morris shifts his position, reading the newspaper

Jean What would you have done if you'd've won?
Morris I'd live out my fantasies. And I'd have this bloody great grin on
  my face, all the time. I wouldn't spend a bloody penny.
Jean No change there then!
Morris Why, what would you do?
Jean I'd go to Hollywood.
Morris Hollywood? I'd rather go to Brid.

Jean You go to Brid then. And then I'd go to Venice. I can just see me sat in Beverly Hills with all the stars. Then when I'd come back I'd kick you out, and get myself a Chippendale!

Morris If you won I'd leave anyway. I couldn't stand it!

Jean No, I wouldn't want to start with somebody else all over again, you only end up being here.

Morris I hope not.

Jean They'd have to give me a fortune to swap you.

Morris Oh ay?

Jean I'd buy a nice big house with a big front lawn and I'd play croquet.

Morris Croquet? Whatever for?

Jean I've never played it.

Morris It's boring.

Jean How do you know?

Morris I'll tell you sommat I'm glad we've not won.

Jean Why?

Morris Well, can you imagine what we'd be like? We can't agree what to do with nothing, how would we go on with all that lot?

Jean I dunno.

Morris Mind you, I know what you'd do. You'd buy a bloody video shop wouldn't you, that's what you'd do.

Jean I'd do that studio tour.

Morris Twenty million.

Jean Yeh.

Morris Twenty million.

Jean We'd never worry about a bill again.

Morris Twenty bloody million.

Jean Don't forget to take that cheque in.

Morris Twenty million.

Jean It's overdue as it is.

Morris I'd be happy with sixty quid.

Jean You wouldn't know what to do with it anyway!

Morris Twenty million, and I didn't even get one number. That's the story of my bloody life that is.

Morris exits with the paper. Jean watches TV

Music: Jim Capaldi's Love Hurts

Black-out

SCENE 2

Jean watches Blind Date

Music fades

Morris enters. He has an outside coat and his security jumper which he dons during the scene

Morris They should ban that.
Jean Why should they?
Morris It's disgusting.
Jean It isn't.
Morris I don't think it should be on the telly.
Jean Why not?
Morris It's pornography.
Jean It isn't.
Morris It is.
Jean How is it?
Morris It's obscene.
Jean It isn't.
Morris It is. It's rotting this nation that. It's polluting minds is that. That's why there's violence on the streets, that's why the hooligan is back. They're protesting about that rubbish.
Jean It's not rubbish!
Morris Look at it.
Jean I'm trying to, but you're in the bloody way.
Morris I can't watch it.
Jean It's only *Blind Date*.
Morris I know what it is.
Jean It's a laugh.
Morris What are they wearing, look what she is wearing? They're all dogs all three of 'em.
Jean Listen who's talking.
Morris They don't even make up their own lines.
Jean They do.
Morris They don't, they don't. It's obscene. They get these bits of kids, put them on the telly, humiliate them in front of millions and then whoosh finished you never hear of any of them again. There are kids

who think the height of achievement in this country is to appear on *Blind Date*. I mean, what a way to meet somebody.

Jean I like it.

Morris "Hello, if you were my tennis coach I'd let you win game set and match with me every time." I mean, come on? Who talks like that? What are they going to talk about for the rest of their lives, forehand top spin?

Jean I like it.

Morris I bet he chooses her, I bet he chooses number three, look at her, oh no, look at her. What's she say?

Jean I don't know, I can't hear it for you.

Morris What did she say?

Jean I can't hear it.

Morris Told you, told you he'd choose number three, look at her, she's seven feet tall, he's a midget. Oh, it's sad, look at it, it's sad. And look at Cilla, what's she wearing?

Jean I didn't know she'd got a limp, did you?

Morris I can't watch it, it's just sad.

Jean Oh, she's got a limp, that number three.

Morris puts on the outdoor coat

Morris I'm going to get off then.

Jean I knew you'd have to go.

Morris I'm only going to be there an hour because I'll be at the hospital till nine.

Jean There's some magazines in the kitchen, take them with you, she likes reading 'em.

Morris I mean, it's not exactly great fun sitting with my mother for an hour, is it?

Jean Your Vera should go.

Morris I mean that's another situation that's in the lap of the gods.

Jean You always look on the black side.

Morris Well, it is.

Jean Oh, by the way, before I forget, I changed your numbers.

Morris Eh?

Jean I changed your numbers.

Morris What for?

Jean Because they were wrong.

Morris Wrong?

Jean Yeh.

Morris Wrong?

Jean Yes!

Morris How can my numbers be wrong?

Jean Well, they were.

Morris I picked 'em, how could they have been wrong?

Jean Well, I looked and...

Morris I don't believe this.

Jean Well, I...

Morris You changed my numbers...

Jean You never have twenty-six.

Morris How could you?

Jean You had twenty-six.

Morris I've spent all week working out that bloody sequence.

Jean Well, I thought...

Morris I've been working out a sequence all week, I've been listening to the dogs bark, counting bloody magpies, looking how many pieces of scrap are stacked in one square yard just to get my numbers. And you've changed the buggers!

Jean I thought it was a mistake.

Morris It is now!

Jean You always have eighteen, don't you?

Morris It's my birthday.

Jean But on your list, you didn't have eighteen, you had twenty-six.

Morris I know.

Jean And I thought, oh, he's made a mistake, he's forgotten his birthday.

Morris How would I forget my own birthday?

Jean Well, you forget nearly everything else.

Morris Do I change yours?

Jean No.

Morris Do I fiddle about with yours?

Jean No.

Morris So don't change mine.

Jean All right, well, I'm sorry.

Morris Yeh, what if twenty-six comes up?

Jean Sorry.

Morris You read about this stuff in the paper, some poor sod in Windermere had his numbers changed and lost four million. I can't believe this, what if twenty-six comes up and we miss the chance?

Jean You've got to get the others and all.

Morris This is just typical, isn't it?

Jean Eighteen might come up.

Morris Oh ay, I can just see that. Pigs might fly and all. I bet six eighteens come up!

Jean Well, it might.

Morris I mean, this is just absolutely typical of you. You have to interfere, you have to change everything. You have to be like my mother. I've already got one mother, Jean. She's dying in hospital, I don't want another one. Wives should always be lovers too, not mothers, lovers. Did you know that?

Jean Is that what you used to play?

Morris You have to change everything I do. I mean, good grief you even tell me what to wear.

Jean Well, it's a good job isn't it?

Morris Is it?

Jean If I didn't say anything you'd be going out dressed up like Coco the bloody Clown.

Morris is exasperated

Morris I don't know, there must be more to life than this!

Jean Go out if you're going, you're late as it is. She'll wonder where you are.

Morris Yes, Mother.

Jean I've got to mother you you're so bloody ridiculous.

Morris is about to depart. He notices the numbers on the TV

Morris Hang on.

Jean What.

Morris Let's just see what's happening.

Jean You have to cause an argument, don't you?

Morris I just want to see if twenty-six comes up.

Jean Oh, leave it, go if you're going.

Morris Just let's see.

Jean What's it at this week?

Morris Eight million.

Jean Get a pen.

Morris Hang on.
Jean First one's coming.
Morris Six.
Jean Six. I've got that.
Morris I have.
Jean Six has been out nearly every week.
Morris Has it?
Jean Seven. No. You have. You've got seven.
Morris I've got seven.
Jean Good start, then.
Morris Told you I felt lucky, didn't I?
Jean Probably not get any more.
Morris Thanks!
Jean Knowing your luck.
Morris Shuttup you!
Jean Ten? No. Low numbers this week, aren't they?
Morris I've got that, I've got that. I've got ten. I've got them three.
Jean That's a tenner.
Morris I'm in here.
Jean Come on eighteen.
Morris Come on eighteen.
Jean Oh, oh… I'm shaking.
Morris Oh, whooooo!
Jean What's happened to it?
Morris Come on.
Jean Come on eighteen.

Jean is animated, she is jumping around

Morris Sit down, woman, you're putting the speck on it. (*He points at the TV*) Oh, look at this, look at this, there's a fault.
Jean Oh no.
Morris A temporary fault.
Jean It's probably with the weather.
Morris A temporary fault.
Jean Bloody hell.
Morris A temporary fault, oh, come on lucky eighteen…
Jean Come on eighteen.
Morris Watch it be twenty-six.

Jean Come on eighteen.

Morris If it's twenty-six I'll kill you I will honest.

Jean It could be eighteen and twenty-six.

Morris Just watch it be twenty-six. Honest, if it's twenty-six I'll die, I will
honestly swing for you if it's twenty-six. Come on eighteen where are
you? Come on!!! If it's twenty-six I will honestly... I don't know what
I'll do.

Jean Look out it's back!!

Black-out

*Suddenly, Morris and Jean are plunged into darkness. There has been a
power cut, both of them are absolutely staggered*

Morris Bloody hell.

Jean What is it?

Morris Arghhh!

Jean Power's gone.

Morris Bloody hell!!

Jean Try the lights.

Morris Bloody power cut.

Jean Oh, what?

Morris Oh no.

Jean Did you pay the electric?

Morris What?

Jean Didn't you pay it?

Morris When?

Jean When I told you.

Morris A bloody power cut?

Jean On Monday.

Morris Monday?

Jean I asked you to pay the bloody thing because we'd got a final demand.

Morris I can't remember.

Jean You forget everything.

Morris This is with you.

Jean How is it?

Morris You spend all we earn on bloody lottery tickets.

Jean It's you, it's you. You should've paid the bill. I asked you, I left the
bill on the table for you.

Morris I can't remember everything.

Jean You can't remember anything!

Morris Get the radio.

Jean What?

Morris The radio, they have the numbers on the radio.

Jean The batteries have gone.

Morris Since when?

Jean Monday, you were listening to the rugby because you didn't want to watch the telly. You were listening to the bloody thing all night. I couldn't sleep because you had it on.

Morris This is just...

Jean I asked you to get some.

Morris On Monday, yeh, don't tell me.

Jean You should've gone to the bloody supermarket but you'd forgot because you missed the bus.

Morris If it's twenty-six after all this I'll hang myself.

Jean Hang on...

Morris and Jean crack into fits of laughter

> *This laughter is supported by the laughter of Annie and Norman. Annie is Jean's younger sister. She is quite an odd-ball and can look slightly larger than life. Similarly, Norman is larger than life. He is wearing quite a belly and is balding heavily*

Morris and Jean are now multimillionaires. Annie and Norman have brought on a bottle of champagne and some glasses. Lights slowly up

Annie (*astonished*) Two million?

Norman I still can't believe it.

Morris You should've seen us in the bloody power cut.

Annie Two million.

Morris It was like Laurel and Hardy!

Jean He still went to see the band though!

Annie Where's the money?

Morris It's upstairs under the bed.

Annie It's not?

Morris It is. You should see the bed. It's nearly three foot off the floor! Can't open the door for cash!

Norman They reckon we'll all know somebody who's won it. That's what they reckon. Sooner or later.

Annie What are you going to do with it?

Jean Spend the bugger.

Norman They reckon sooner or later we'll all know somebody.

Morris We're not doing anything just yet.

Jean We're having a conservatory.

Annie You should flit, you can't live around here!

Jean I've always wanted a conservatory on.

Morris We've had the bathroom done.

Annie Already?

Jean First thing. I says, Morris, right, spa bath.

Annie Bloody hell. Spending it like water.

Norman Just four winners then?

Morris You know she changed the numbers.

Norman I bet you went bloody mad.

Annie Aren't you flitting?

Jean Are we hell.

Morris We're going to have some alterations.

Jean I'm having all the house done!

Annie Oh, you can't stop here, can they, Norman?

Norman Get yourself off.

Annie You can't stop here. It's not right.

Jean No, we're staying.

Annie Oh no, I wouldn't want to stop here.

Norman Leave 'em, let 'em do what they want.

Annie I'd want somewhere different.

Norman A multimillionaire eh? What's it feel like?

Morris Well…

Norman A lot bloody better.

Morris Well, yeh…

Norman What are you doing about work?

Morris About what?

Norman I'd never work again!

Annie We nearly won a month ago you know? We had two numbers, and all the others were just out by one.

Norman Couldn't believe it.

Morris No?

Norman Two numbers and all the others out by one.

Morris Well, there you go…

Norman Mind you, I told her, it's a lottery, isn't it?

Morris It is, isn't it?

Norman Two numbers and all the rest were just out by one.

Annie You're going on a world trip, aren't you?

Jean Los Angeles on Saturday. We're going to make it crack.

Annie Listen to her, she's like Joan Collins.

Jean Well, it's about time we had sommat.

Morris I reckon Jean'll have spent it by the weekend!

Jean I can try!

Norman Flying first class?

Jean Why, is there another class?

Norman It's all change now!

Annie You should get a new car. I mean, that one's been in the garage for years, hasn't it. Get a Jag or sommat.

Morris Well, we'll have to see.

Annie Get a new 'un.

Jean Morris doesn't drive much.

Annie He's thinking about getting one.

Norman Just thinking.

Annie They're laying 'em off at their place, aren't they?

Norman Two hundred got to go.

Morris Like you said, you might never work again?

Annie I mean, if he gets made redundant I don't know what we'll do.

Norman Two hundred they're going to get rid of.

Morris He'll fall on his feet will Norman, always has done!

Norman Two hundred. Rationalizing they call it.

Annie Mind you, I says to him, we should be all right now we've got a millionaire in the family eh?

Morris Ay, we're having a conservatory on!

Norman Should look good.

Morris All that back's going to go.

Norman Looks good I think.

Morris Two hundred eh?

Norman Looking good though.

Jean Come on, Annie, I'll show you the spa bath.

Annie Bloody hell.

Jean I'm going to show our Annie...

Annie and Jean are preparing to exit from stage. Norman and Morris are down stage

Annie Can I have a go in it?
Jean If you want.
Annie Is it bubbly?
Jean Bubbly? It's like being in a washing machine.

Annie and Jean exit

Silence

Norman Uh oooh!
Morris Eh?
Norman Bloody hell.
Morris What?
Norman I look at you and I think. Bloody hell. I think bloody hell, my brother-in-law is worth a fortune.
Morris Ay, well.
Norman And you look just the same.
Morris Do I?
Norman Not a bloody worry eh?
Morris That's right.
Norman Not a worry in the world.
Morris I wouldn't go that far.
Norman Get away, man.
Morris Well, anyway…
Norman They send you for counselling or sommat, don't they? I saw this thing in the paper about 'em sending some poor sod for counselling who couldn't handle it. If you can't handle it just hand it over to me and Annie, we'll spend it for you.
Morris I bet you would.
Norman They invest it for you and that?
Morris We've seen an adviser.
Norman Should be able to live off the interest, shouldn't you?
Morris To be honest, I haven't given it much thought. It's such a surprise you know what I mean? I mean, I've been thinking about doing all sorts, having a change, and then this has come up and thrown me!
Norman Bloody hell, I'd be counting it. What do they do? Give it you in a cheque or what?
Morris No, they bring it in one pound coins.
Norman What, in a lorry?
Morris That's right.

Norman I look at you and you don't look much different.
Morris Ay, well.
Norman Came at the right time and all, didn't it?
Morris Well, this is what I'm saying...
Norman Annie said you and Jean have been a bit...?
Morris There's a lot of guilt in our house, Norman.
Norman She told me you were working every hour God sent.
Morris Another life now, Norman.
Norman Mind you, you should hear me and her.
Morris Oh yeh.
Norman Bloody chaos half the time. She's round the bloody bend Annie, you know?
Morris Eh?
Norman Bloody hell!
Morris Yeh, well...

A beat

Norman No, well...
Morris It's a bit...
Norman I know.
Morris Twenty-two years.
Norman For better or for worse.
Morris Absolutely.
Norman And it doesn't get any easier, does it?
Morris That's right.
Norman Mind you, this is like starting again, isn't it?
Morris You reckon?
Norman Oh ay. Somebody up there likes you, mate!
Morris Yeh?
Norman This is what you need, isn't it? This'll sort you out. I'll tell you this, if I won I'd leave her tomorrow. I even tried one of them scratch and sniff cards the other day.
Morris Scratch and win you mean?
Norman Well, I scratched, but I didn't get a bloody sniff.
Morris Ay, they're making some money, aren't they?
Norman But this is like being born again is this. Just think about it, you can do exactly as you want. It's like having a new life, mate. You can do just what you want now. You'll be fishing every day God sends.

Morris Ay and I'll probably still not catch owt!

Norman If you wanted to go back to the clubs it's just a phone call away. Morris Sod "the millionaire drummer". Get back with Connie Wilde's band, you'd pack 'em in now.

Morris It's a thought.

Norman Oh ay, you'd be in there now!

Morris Twenty-two years of married bliss though!

Norman This is the chance to do just as you want. You could buy your Vera out of that hairdressing job.

Morris She's on about flitting. Doug's just got a job with Group Four.

Norman It's all waiting for you, Morris.

Morris Brave new world eh?

Norman Have you told your mam?

Morris Not yet.

Norman She'll have a bloody stroke.

Morris I hope not, Norman, she's already had four!

Morris and Norman laugh. Music: Four Seasons' Storm in a Teacup

Black-out

Scene 3

A hospital ward

Molly, Morris's mother, is in a large hospital bed. She is in her late seventies, and is quite ill, yet in a strange way also quite alert

Morris enters, wearing a short anorak. He looks at his mother and stands in silence

Morris All right?

Molly Late, aren't you?

Morris Couldn't get parked.

Molly It's nearly ten o'clock.

Morris No, it's only seven...

Molly Nearly ten o'clock.

Morris Anyway. (*He sits beside her*)

Molly I thought you weren't coming.

Morris Yeh. I'm always late, aren't I?

Molly Always have been.

Morris That's right.

Molly You were always late as a kid.

Morris Yeh.

Molly Always late.

Morris I know.

Molly Always been a little bugger.

Morris I know.

Molly Never been satisfied? No matter what we did for you you were never satisfied.

Morris Just rest, Mam.

Molly And swearing.

Morris Who?

Molly Always swearing.

Morris Me?

Molly Bloody this, bloody that.

Morris I wasn't, was I?

Molly Always swearing.

Morris I got it from you.

Molly I never.

Morris Not much.

Molly We were at Blackpool and me and your dad had just come to look at the weather. It was throwing it down, can you remember?

Morris You tell me every time I come.

Molly And it was throwing it down.

Morris That's right.

Molly And you came down and you just stood there, in that lumber jacket your gran had bought you, and you said: "I'm not going out in that, it's pissing it down."

Morris I can't remember.

Molly Pissing it down, is what you said.

Morris No, I can't remember.

Molly I said to your dad, where's he got that from?

Morris No idea.

Molly Always swearing.

Morris And I've been swearing ever since.

Molly You have.

A beat

Morris So how are you then?
Molly And your dad never swore.
Morris No.
Molly Not at home anyway.
Morris No.
Molly Never swore.
Morris So how are you feeling then?
Molly I don't know what he did at work, but at home, he never swore.
Morris That's right.
Molly Vera's been.
Morris Has she?
Molly This afternoon.
Morris Oh right.
Molly Her hair looks a bugger.
Morris Oh right.
Molly I don't know what she's done with it. All over the shop. Looks like a bird's shit on her head.
Morris I know the style.
Molly She doesn't look well.
Morris She looks off it then, does she?
Molly I look better than her.

A beat

Morris We've had a bit of good news, Mam.
Molly Boiling at night.
Morris Me and Jean have had a bit of good news.
Molly That's good then.
Morris Yeh, we've had a bit of luck.
Molly I wish I had.
Morris You will have.
Molly I thought she couldn't have any more?
Morris No, Mam.
Molly What's that thing she's got?
Morris It's endometriosis, Mam, but...
Molly They never called it that when I couldn't have any more.
Morris It's not that...

Molly You'll be lost without 'em.
Morris Yeh, yeh, that's right.
Molly I mean all I've got now is you and our Vera.
Morris That's right.
Molly Our Vera looks shocking.
Morris Got a new haircut, hasn't she?
Molly It suits her and all.
Morris We, er ... we've come into a bit of money, Mam.
Molly You have?
Morris Me and Jean.
Molly It'll come in handy for the baby then.
Morris (*whispering*) We've won the Lottery.
Molly The what?
Morris The Lottery.
Molly Pottery?
Morris (*laughing with her*) No, we've won two million on the Lottery.
Molly What?
Morris Yeh.
Molly Pissing hell!
Morris Yeh, I know. We're millionaires now, Mam, me and Jean.
Molly Well, you lucky sods.
Morris I know.
Molly I've never won owt!
Morris We're going to take good care of you.
Molly I won forty quid on the bingo and that's going back.
Morris You needn't worry about owt.
Molly I don't want going in a home.
Morris I know.
Molly I'd sooner stay here.
Morris Can't stay here, can you?
Molly I'd sooner stay here.
Morris Ay, we've got all the money in the world now, Mam.
Molly Well, it'll not do me any good.
Morris It will.
Molly Too late for me!
Morris We're going to America.
Molly What for?
Morris A break.
Molly A break, you should try coming in here... You want to be careful.

Morris I will.

Molly And take plenty of clean clothes.

Morris I bet you wish you could come, don't you?

Molly I don't.

Morris Our Vera's going to see to you, and then we're going to get you somewhere nice.

Molly I don't want leaving.

Morris I wouldn't leave you, would I?

Molly You left me for Jean.

Morris Mam?

Molly You left me then.

Morris I love you, Mam, you know that.

Molly A millionaire?

Morris You know I do.

Molly I knew you when you used to swear.

Morris I swore when I won it.

Molly Did you?

Morris I bloody did.

Molly Two million?

Morris That's right.

Molly Oh, I could spend that. I could be down the market and spend that, I could. I'd give that some hammer on the veg stall. Look at you? All that money and you couldn't have a shave.

Morris Well, you know...?

Molly I knew you when you had nothing.

Morris I'll not change, Mam.

Molly Better not had.

Morris It's nowt, all that money, is it?

A beat

Molly Look at you.

Morris What?

Molly All that money and you couldn't buy me any bloody flowers, you're a bloody mess!!!

Music

Black-out

SCENE 4

The Beverly Hills Hotel. Early evening

A Waiter is placing some large flowers on top of a chest of drawers

He is about to exit, when Jean enters. She has a number of obviously expensive shopping bags, boxes and the like. She has just returned from shopping

Waiter Oh, I'm sorry! I was just refreshing your room!

Jean Oh, it's all right love, I'm buggered. We've been up and down Rodeo Drive a hundred times.

Waiter Have you had a good day?

Jean Yeh, but there's no air is there?

Waiter Only smog. Is your room OK?

Jean Well, it's not what we expected.

Waiter I think you got the last one. We're rather busy at the moment.

Jean You're telling me! I had to fight my way through the bloody foyer. I've never seen so many cigars. I can't stand the smell.

Waiter Is there anything I can get you? Room service? A drink or anything?

Jean Oh, I could kill a shandy.

Waiter A shandy, what is that?

Jean Beer and lemonade.

Waiter OK, no problem. I'll fix that myself. One shandy coming up. Anything to eat?

Jean No, I've had a burger.

Waiter Are you Australian?

Jean English.

Waiter English great. Anthony Hopkins uh...

Jean From Yorkshire.

Waiter Yorkshire?

Jean Yeh.

Waiter Where is that?

Jean The North.

Waiter Oh right, near Edinburgh?

Jean No, near York. Do you know York? It's very old. Oh it's lovely is York.

Waiter No, sorry, we don't have old here.

Jean It's very big, like your Texas.

Waiter Get out of here, what?

Jean So, is this where all the stars stay?

Waiter When they're in town.

Jean I wonder if any of them have stayed in here? Probably Shirley Temple going on the space?

Waiter You were lucky to get a room.

Jean Yeh, I'm very lucky.

Waiter I think Tom Cruise is staying here tonight.

Jean You're joking?

Waiter No way.

Jean Tom Cruise?

Waiter Sure.

Jean In this hotel? What number is he?

Waiter I couldn't tell you.

Jean Tom Cruise? I might do a bit of sleep walking.

Waiter That's what they all say!

Jean Mind you, I like Clint the best.

Waiter He's great.

Jean Have you seen *In the Line of Fire*?

Waiter Sure.

Jean I've seen all Clint's films.

Waiter Yeh?

Jean Did you like it?

Waiter Pardon me?

Jean *In the Line of Fire*?

Waiter Yeh, it was an OK movie.

Jean When he was running with the car. Oooh eh?

Waiter Yeh?

Jean Oh yeh.

Waiter Clint's staying here. I've served Clint on several occasions.

Jean Really?

Waiter Sure.

Jean He's sixty, isn't he?

Waiter Yeh, but he looks real great. Don't you think?

Jean He does. I wonder what number he's in?

Waiter Are you here alone?

Jean I wish. With my husband.

Waiter Is he sixty too?
Jean He acts like he is.
Waiter And he looks like Clint?
Jean Well...?
Waiter So, is he with the police?
Jean No, he's a night-watchman really!
Waiter OK, so one shandy. Beer with lemon. Would you like Bud, Becks, Michelob?

Morris enters. He is dressed in shorts and a Californian-style shirt. The heat is getting to him

Jean Do you want a shandy, Clint?
Morris I'll have a Coke.
Waiter Sure, Diet or with the E numbers?
Morris Diet.
Jean Tom Cruise comes here.
Morris I'll have what he has then.
Jean There's a do on down there.
Morris I know. I've just seen Jack Nicholson.
Jean Where?
Morris Down by the pool.
Jean Why didn't you shout me?
Morris I'm three hundred yards away.
Jean Oh, Jack Nicholson?
Morris Yeh, just saw him down there.
Jean You could've got me.
Morris Oh, that would've looked good, wouldn't it. Jack? Have you got a minute, come and meet Jean she works in the same industry. Film distribution.
Waiter OK, one shandy, one Coke. I'll be about five minutes.

The Waiter exits

Jean Fancy not telling me about Jack Nicholson?
Morris Why, what would you have said? Hello, Jack?
Jean I know but.
Morris Hello, Jack, I sell a lot of your videos.
Jean Is he tall?

Morris Taller than he is on our telly.
Jean They all come here, he says.
Morris They're all down there, must be a do or sommat.
Jean I've not seen anybody famous.
Morris You've seen Bing Crosby's house.
Jean Only half of it.
Morris You've seen where Marilyn's buried.
Jean I saw Michael Douglas.
Morris When?
Jean In that perfume shop.
Morris That wasn't Michael Douglas.
Jean It was.
Morris It looked more like Michael bloody Aspel.
Jean It was Michael Douglas. I should know. You never watch the films
anyway. Two minutes and you're asleep with your slippers off. I mean
talk about sensorama? The bloody pong sometimes.

A beat

Morris Yeh, they're all down there.
Jean Fancy not shouting me to see Jack?
Morris I've just seen Demi Moore and all.
Jean Is she nice?
Morris Well, she didn't speak but...
Jean I don't like her. She's the same in everything.
Morris They're all the same in everything.
Jean There's no air is there!
Morris I've just been in the bog with Jean-Claude Van Damme.
Jean You never?
Morris I have. I splashed his shoes and all.
Jean You never.
Morris And he never said owt!
Jean Moss!
Morris Never said a word.
Jean Are you joking?
Morris No. I stood there, splashed him and then gave him one of my
looks. Never uttered a word.
Jean Are you serious?
Morris No, I'm pulling your bloody leg, you nit!

Jean I thought…

A beat

Morris Saw Jack Nicholson though. I nodded but I didn't get owt back.

A beat

Jean He probably didn't recognize you without your uniform on.
Morris That'd be it.

A beat

   I'm tired out.
Jean We've covered some ground, haven't we?
Morris There's nowt else left to see, is there?

A beat

Jean Just Disneyland.
Morris Eh?
Jean We'll go to Disneyland tomorrow.
Morris Eh?
Jean Disneyland.
Morris When?
Jean Tomorrow?
Morris It's miles out, isn't it?
Jean Hire a car again.
Morris Well?
Jean Don't you want to go?
Morris Well, I'm not…
Jean I thought you fancied it?
Morris Well, I did.
Jean Be a laugh that…
Morris Yeh, but…
Jean I've always wanted to go.
Morris Don't you think we might be a bit old?
Jean It'll be a laugh.
Morris I dunno.

Jean Oh yeh.
Morris I just think it might look a bit odd.
Jean Who to?
Morris I dunno.
Jean How can it look odd then?
Morris I just feel a bit…
Jean You have to spoil everything, don't you?
Morris No, it's just…
Jean You do.
Morris I don't.
Jean Aren't you enjoying it?
Morris Course I am.
Jean Well then?
Morris I just, well, dunno about it to be honest.
Jean Why?
Morris Because.
Jean Oh, we're back to not saying what you mean, are we?
Morris No, but.
Jean It's only for a laugh, isn't it, to say we've done it?
Morris I just don't think we should go.
Jean What?
Morris I don't think we should.
Jean Why?
Morris Let's leave it.
Jean Let's not.
Morris Don't scratch at scabs, Jean.
Jean We're two thousand miles away from home, now what's wrong?

A beat

Morris The furthest I've ever been is Torremolinos.
Jean Oh, Morris, you know how to kill it, don't you?
Morris Can you remember?
Jean We stayed at the Angela.
Morris What the bloody hell am I doing here?
Jean Nice hotel.
Morris We had a sea view.
Jean That's right.
Morris It cost us an extra fifty quid. But we were determined to have that sea view.

Jean That's right.
Morris All three of us in one bed.

A beat

Jean Don't!
Morris I miss her.
Jean Six years now.
Morris I know.
Jean So what do you want to do?
Morris Anything but Disneyland.
Jean Yeh, sorry.
Morris It wasn't your fault…
Jean I wasn't even thinking…
Morris It just gets to me at times.

Jean tries to lift the atmosphere

Jean I mean look at us. We're in the Beverly Hills Hotel. I've got a shandy
and you've got a Diet Coke. Aren't we pathetic?

They share a laugh

Morris Yeh…
Jean We should've had some of this years ago. But you never wanted to
come.
Morris We couldn't afford to come here.
Jean You were satisfied with fishing in Brid. Bloody Brid. Fifteen years
we went to Brid.
Morris Brid's all right.
Jean It took me six months to get you on a plane to Spain.
Morris Don't knock Brid.
Jean I'm not.
Morris We had some good times at Brid.
Jean It's not the same though, is it?
Morris I bet Jack Nicholson's never been to Brid? Or Demi Moore. Or
Clint. I bet they've never had fish 'n' chips out of the paper?
Jean They haven't lived, have they?
Morris Have they hell.

Jean I bet they've never stayed at Mucky Maureen's at Skipsea either.
Morris Definitely not.
Jean They'd've known about it if they had.
Morris I bet they've never been caravanning?
Jean Definitely not.
Morris Where have these people been?
Jean Sad, isn't it?
Morris They must lead such sheltered lives.
Jean All those sex orgies, and cocaine and they've never really lived.
Morris Well, they did that song about it, didn't they?
Jean Which?
Morris One about Vegas and unknown places and seeing things a woman
    shouldn't see…
Jean (*helping him*) I've been to paradise, but I've never been to Brid.

Laughter between Morris and Jean. A beat

    Where do you fancy next?
Morris We can't be spending it just like that.
Jean Course we can.
Morris We'll be all right here till Saturday.
Jean No chance, where do you want to go? Venice?
Morris Venice?
Jean Rome?
Morris Eh?
Jean New York. Miami!
Morris No…
Jean They have fishing there, sharks and all sorts. Oh, I fancy that!
Morris Bloody hell, Jean, you were bad enough with a Marks and
    Spencer's card. But this is ridiculous!
Jean Venice.
Morris Hang on.
Jean Venice. I've always wanted to go.
Morris Bloody Venice?
Jean Right then.
Morris Woow, hang on.
Jean What's up, do you feel guilty?
Morris Well?
Jean Well, do you?

Morris Well, yeh.

Jean I don't.

Morris Don't you?

Jean What would Annie and Norman have done if they'd've won? Stopped at home for fear of feeling guilty?

Morris Well, no...

Jean Well then?

Morris I mean, why us?

Jean What are we supposed to do? Stop living?

Morris It's not that...

Jean We're supposed to start living.

Morris I know.

Jean Listen, my mother never saw anything, did she? Not anything.

Morris I know that.

Jean When she was seventy-one our Annie took her to Leeds. Can you remember her going to Leeds?

Morris Yeh.

Jean They went on the bus from Barnsley. For her birthday.

Morris I know...

Jean She never stopped talking about that. Going to the big city. Wait till I tell some of them at the social, that's what she said. Seventy-one years and she'd finally plucked up enough courage to go to Leeds. And I'm not exaggerating.

Morris I know you're not.

Jean Jesus, that makes me...

Morris I know.

Jean I could scream, when I think about it. Bloody Leeds!

Morris I know.

Jean She thought she was the bee's knees because she'd been to British Home Stores. And when she died I remember somebody saying, she went all over the place her. Who did she think she was, she was always galavanting off. She went once. I tried to get her on a Wallace Arnold trip to Eastbourne but she said it was too far. So why do you feel guilty? We're not lucky; yes it could have been anybody. But we've earned this! Look, how many nights did you play your last gig?

Morris Hundreds.

Jean Well then.

Morris What?

Jean How many nights did you say "That's it, never again"?

Morris Hundreds.

Jean How many nights do you sit looking at that scrap yard?

Morris Too many.

Jean How many times do you think there's got to be more than this?

Morris I know, you're right.

Jean Look at that one-armed pianist in Scarborough?

Morris Barbara Lucas?

Jean That's her.

Morris What about her?

Jean You deserve a hundred grand for working with her.

Morris And the rest.

Jean And that MC in Teeside?

Morris Tonight and tonight only, Sweet Sensation.

Jean *Sad Sweet Dreamer.*

Morris Awful night!

Jean You deserve a hundred grand for working there.

Morris Probably more actually!

Jean Well then?

Morris It's like a bloody dream though.

Jean Right, sup your Coke, Clint.

Morris Where are we going?

Jean We're going to Venice.

Morris When?

Jean Now!

Morris and Jean exit

Music

Black-out

SCENE 5

Home. Evening. Christmas

*Norman enters. He is wearing a paper crown, for Christmas. He stands
and looks toward where the conservatory is built*

Annie enters. She is clearly worse for a few drinks and has a handful of

letters with her. She has just left the kitchen, and is full of Christmas spirit.
She looks at the conservatory and then moves to sit

Annie You seen the conservatory?

Norman Can't miss it. There's no garden left.

Annie They should've flitted.

Norman It'll not take him long to cut the lawn, that's one good thing.

Annie Why's that?

Norman There's only a square yard of it. If they have two sparrows on the lawn it'll be a severe case of overcrowding.

Annie What do you think about Morris?

Norman Well, he's cut his gardening commitments.

Annie Changed, don't you think.

Norman No.

Annie Oh, he has. He's a nervous wreck.

Norman Is he hell.

Annie Jean's the same but he's changed.

Norman Well, Jean's cooking's not changed, has it?

Annie She's never been a good cook our Jean.

Norman She cooks the only food I've ever been scared of.

Annie And cheap sherry, isn't it? Have you read these?

Norman What are they?

Annie Letters.

Norman I can see that.

Annie They should've never given out their address. If we win we're keeping shtum!

Norman They always had cheap sherry, didn't they?

Annie Have you seen these?

Norman Does she know you've got 'em?

Annie Well, we're family, aren't we?

Norman You shouldn't be reading them.

Annie (*still absorbed in the letters*) Venice sounds nice, doesn't it?

Norman Fancy coming back on the Orient Express? Bloody hell, throwing money away.

Annie Did you like your present?

Norman What present?

Annie Exactly.

Norman I expected a car or sommat.

Annie Exactly.

Norman I thought, I'll play it all coy and when they give us the car I'll cry and kiss Morris. I got the same thing that I've had for the past six years.

Annie And me.

Norman Bloody soap-on-a-rope.

Annie Did you see what I'd got?

Norman I haven't used last year's yet. I've got a bathroom cabinet full of model soap sports cars. I could start a shop up.

Annie And after all we'd bought them?

Norman I bet I've got nearly thirty foot of rope?

Annie Fifty quid that food mixer, you know?

Norman He's always had his pockets sewn up has Morris.

Annie Oh, listen to this…

Norman Should you be reading them?

Annie "Dear Whoever, My little girl is in need of a serious operation."

Norman Don't be reading that…

Annie (*still reading*) "We have been attempting to secure funds for the past few months. If you can spare anything to help us please do so. Yours Jenny Wright aged five and Mummy".

Norman Bloody hell.

Annie Oh.

Norman Poor sods.

Annie I wonder if they've sent anything.

Norman Poor little sod.

Annie Do you think…

Norman Probably sent 'em a soap-on-a-rope.

Annie Oh, there's one here from Connie Wilde.

Norman What's she want then?

Annie Just that she saw them in the paper.

Norman There's always been something going on there.

Annie They'll all come out of the woodwork now.

Norman Bloody hangers-on, sickening!

Annie Fancy writing?

Norman People'll do owt.

Annie (*still reading*) Oh, listen to this.

Norman Don't be reading them when they come in!

Annie Oh, this is very good. It just says, "I hope you die you lucky bastards!"

Norman I sent that!

Morris enters, from the kitchen

Morris Another Christmas over.

Norman That's right. Lovely and all.

Morris I enjoy the tea better than the dinner.

Norman She can still cook, Morris. That's one good thing.

Morris Not bad, was it? We were thinking of getting somebody in. But Jean wanted to...

Annie (*still reading*) Oh, one here wants to send her grandad on a world cruise. Oh. She's only seven. Have you read it? Awwwh!

Morris I can't read 'em, I fill up!

Annie He's got cancer and she wants to send him on a holiday to make him better.

Norman Oh, give it a miss.

Annie Awwwh, isn't it awful?

Morris We're not sure which are genuine, you see?

Norman Somebody helped that little lass out with leukaemia, didn't they? I reckon that was a lottery winner. Somebody just gave 'em seventy grand. I mean they need it, don't they? There's bloody hospitals with no beds, I think all the lottery winners should put sommat in a hospital fund, instead of all them bloody holidays.

Morris What, instead of the Government you mean?

Norman Well, this lot aren't interested, are they? I tell you sommat I bet we wouldn't get thirteen million for my grandad's letters.

Annie He was a funny old sod your grandad so you never know.

Norman Bloody opera, fifty-five million? Robbing the poor to pay the rich, that's what it is.

Morris Get away.

Norman It is. I tell you this, they ought to limit the prizes and all. A million, a millionaire a day, I think that'd be better. Eight million a week, make somebody a millionaire every day. If I won I'd give it away I would.

Morris It's funny, when you've got it you don't want to spend it.

Annie We know that.

Norman So what sort of interest do you make a week?

Morris It's no use asking me.

Norman I worked it out, didn't I? I told her. Two grand a week. Two grand a week in interest alone!!

Jean enters, tired and hassled

Jean All done.

Annie Awwwh.

Jean Don't read them, Annie.

Annie I'm only looking.

Jean Don't read them.

Annie I was only having a look.

Jean Yeh, well, it's not right. I haven't had time to look through them yet.

Annie Who are you sending money to, then?

Jean Nobody yet.

Annie Why?

Jean Because. I haven't had a look.

Annie I'd send the lot, wouldn't you, Norman?

Norman I'm just happy with my soap-on-a-rope.

Jean We've had that many.

Annie I'd send, would you?

Jean Well, you've always spent money like water.

Norman Well, I would, yeh but...

Jean We've just got to sort things out yet.

Norman She's never liked parting with money, have you, Jean?

Jean It's not that...

Annie What is it then?

Jean We've got to get sorted yet!

Annie Well, you haven't spent much on Christmas presents, have you? So you've made a saving there.

Jean What do you mean?

Annie I'm just saying the presents are a bit down this year. I mean, me and Norman have made an effort with you and we haven't got anything back.

Jean What did you expect?

Annie Well?

Jean We don't want to spoil anybody.

Annie Well, you've not done that, that is for sure! None of the family have seen any of it.

Norman Morris's mother has.

Morris We didn't want to go mad.

Annie Well, like I say...

Morris It would've been no good spoiling everybody, would it?

Norman Well, you could've tried.

Annie I thought we might have had a little treat but I was obviously wrong.

Morris We were thinking about it.

Annie Thinking's no good, is it? What are you waiting for, we could've been off to Rhodes this Christmas.

Norman She doesn't mean what she's saying, Jean, when she's had a sherry she'll say owt!

Annie I do. I think it's a disgrace. I think they could have at least bought us sommat decent, I mean we've spent more on them and you're out of bloody work. I think it's bloody disgusting to be honest!

Jean I think you'd better go.

Annie I think it's bloody shocking.

Jean I think you'd better go, Annie.

Annie That's the trouble with you two, you can't talk to you. You think you're bloody it.

Jean You'd better go.

Morris Hey, come on, we can talk this out.

Jean Go.

Annie You thought you were special when you had nothing. I don't know who you think you are now?

Morris Now, Annie, you don't mean that.

Annie I do.

Morris Hey, come on, let's all have another sherry and get this sorted.

Annie I mean, Morris thought he was bloody Elvis when he was in that group. He was a right laughing stock. I mean, we all knew there was sommat going on, and now she's writing bloody letters to you. I wouldn't have that!

Jean What are you on about?

Annie After all we've done for you.

Jean After all you've done for us? We haven't seen you for six months. Then when we won you were on the phone every ten bloody minutes.

Morris Who wants a sherry? Norman?

Norman I'd better not.

Morris Annie, sherry?

Norman I think she's had enough!

Annie I tell you this much if I go I'll never come back here again.

Morris Jean?

Jean Go then.

Annie And your bloody conservatory looks a bugger. You've ruined that back garden.

Jean Just go, Annie.

Annie You want to get some of them letters looked at, you do.

Jean I will do.

Annie I bet Connie Wilde finishes up getting more than we do.

Jean What's she got to do with this?

Annie I bet she does, with all her "good luck" and "all the best". She's a bloody mess.

Morris Hang on.

Jean Why didn't you tell me she'd written in?

Morris I was going to.

Jean Oh right.

Annie We're struggling to keep the bloody lights on in our house and you couldn't even buy us a decent Christmas present. I tell you this much, you can stick it. You can stick all your money because we don't bloody want it. Do we, Norman?

Norman Well...?

Annie Stick it up your arse! Come on, you!

Annie exits

Norman moves to exit

Morris Sorry.

Norman Whole new life eh?

Norman exits

Jean Why didn't you tell me about this letter?

Morris Jean?

Jean I told you not to go and see that bloody band.

Morris It's not my fault that she wrote in, is it? I didn't ask to be in the bloody paper. I didn't ask to win the damn thing.

Jean I knew sommat'd happen if she saw you again!

Morris Just leave it.

Jean She's like a bad penny.

Morris We've had a good day, your Annie's a bit highly strung, it's bloody Christmas, just leave it.

Jean Our bloody Annie's got nothing to do with her writing to you.

Morris She hasn't written to me, has she?

Jean Oh, don't give me that.

Morris I said this would happen.

Jean She's always been jealous.

Morris I said, didn't I?

Jean She can't bear anybody having anything.

Morris Can we forget about this please, there's nothing there.

Jean And our Annie?

Morris Your Annie's a bloody nuisance and she always has been.

Jean She knows all about my situation and she begrudges us a bit of
pleasure. I mean it's only two million, isn't it? She's always been like
it, hasn't she? She's got her own kids and they hardly ever come home.

Morris This is just what I said...

Jean And Norman, what did she see in him?

Morris I said this.

Jean What?

Morris Look at us at the airport.

Jean What about us?

Morris That near miss.

Jean What near miss?

Morris There was a bloody plane about three inches away from us when
we were coming out of LAX.

Jean There wasn't a near miss.

Morris What was it then?

Jean It was just close.

Morris Close? Close is two miles away.

Jean Oh, leave it!

Morris We were that close I could smell the pilot's breath.

Jean Oh, don't start.

Morris And what about Venice? That accident?

Jean What accident?

Morris That boat with the glass on it, the bus went past and a sheet of glass
fell off, didn't you see it? It just missed us, straight into the Grand Canal.
Could've took our bloody heads off.

Jean I never saw that.

Morris I bet we get a plague of frogs in that bloody conservatory.

Jean She's always been the same our Annie. And I said we should've
bought 'em sommat decent.

Morris I knew there'd be bloody arguments. I'm pig sick of arguments.

Jean You're the one who makes them! Fancy not telling me about that
letter!

Morris Christmas and look at us!

Jean begins to look through the chest of drawers

Jean Have you moved my stuff?
Morris What stuff?
Jean My numbers.
Morris What numbers?
Jean My lottery whatsit!
Morris What for?
Jean To check 'em.
Morris You've not entered again, have you?
Jean Why not?
Morris Why have you entered again?
Jean There's a twelve million roll over.
Morris I don't believe that you've entered again.
Jean Why not?
Morris I don't believe you've entered again…
Jean It's Christmas.
Morris What if we win?
Jean Oh shurrup!
Morris Don't you think two million's enough?
Jean It's just sommat to do.
Morris Jean, Jean, honestly, honestly. I can't for the life of me think why
     you've entered again. I just don't believe it. This is tempting fate this is,
     this is just bloody stupid! If we win again nobody'll talk to us.

Jean clicks on the TV and sits down

Jean Morris, calm down.
Morris This'll bring bad luck, this will.
Jean Why will it?
Morris Because it does.
Jean Does it hell.
Morris There'll be a plague on our bloody house.
Jean We won't win.
Morris I can just see it…
Jean Nobody is that bloody lucky.
Morris You'll not be able to move for hate mail. I mean, if we win again

I'll have a nervous bloody breakdown, I will. I think I'm going to die any minute now, and if you win again that's it, that's the end, that's all our bloody luck gone. Forget it!

Jean watches the TV and notices her numbers

Jean Oh look, six... I've got that!

Music: Hot Chocolate's You Win Again

Fade to Black-out

CURTAIN

ACT II

SCENE 1

Graveyard. Four months later. A dismal drizzling day

The bare space is now littered with a number of wooden tulips. The red tulips stand out against the colouring in the set

Music: Sweet Sensation's Sad Sweet Dreamer

Jean and Morris are both dressed in black, sombre, funereal clothes. They are at Morris's mother's funeral

Jean Lousy things.
Morris Funerals?
Jean Urgghh!!
Morris Yeh.
Jean Lousy.
Morris One of the few certainties.
Jean Oh, don't.
Morris Well, it is!
Jean It doesn't bear thinking about.
Morris Yeh, it's one of the few things you can rely on.
Jean I don't think about it.
Morris A safe bet every time.
Jean Nice service wasn't it?
Morris I'd put my money on death. A dead cert...
Jean Nice service.
Morris To coin a phrase.
Jean Don't make jokes here.
Morris Strange world, isn't it, when death's the only thing you can be sure about?
Jean Do you think there's something else?
Morris Where?

Jean On the other side?

Morris Well, I hope so, because we're not going to get through fourteen
million on this side, are we?

Jean We can try though.

Morris I hope there's a Marks and Spencer's on the other side, or you'll
be lost. Life without Marks would be purgatory for you, wouldn't it?

Jean It'll not be like this though, will it?

Morris Not with any luck!

Jean What do you mean?

Morris Well, there's one thing for sure, there'll be no death. We'll have
crossed that one!

Jean That's a relief.

Morris Everybody will be already dead, won't they? Just think, shopping
in Marks and Debenhams for the rest of eternity?

Jean Yeh, sounds good.

Morris I think I'd rather stay on this side come to think of it.

A beat

Jean I did like your mam you know?

Morris Did you?

Jean She was a funny old bird but...

Morris How do you know, you never spoke to her!

Jean She was a good woman though.

Morris Why is it now?

Jean It's fate, isn't it? It's all mapped out.

Morris We didn't have a penny fifteen years ago. Only had two million
four days ago.

Jean That's luck, I suppose.

Morris Bad luck, you mean.

Jean Morris!

Morris Bad luck.

Jean Just because something good happens it doesn't always mean
something bad happens.

Morris What are we doing here then? Fishing? I mean fourteen million,
Jean, is bloody ridiculous.

Jean It's not my fault!

Morris There's blokes in the pub who come up to me and ask me to shake
their hands. They think some of the luck'll rub off. There was a woman

the other day who'd driven down from Berwick just to look at our house, did you know that? She saw me in the garden, asked me if I'd stroke her face. I felt like the Pope. She said her mother was going in for an operation and she wanted a bit of good luck. I told her bad luck follows good luck. She asked where you were.

Jean What did you say?

Morris I told her you were doing "Spot the Ball" for a charity.

Jean Ha ha.

Morris You know we need to get sorted?

Jean How do you mean?

Morris I mean, we need to talk.

Jean What about?

Morris All sorts, all this!

Jean What sort of all sorts?

Morris Liquorice bloody Allsorts.

Jean Don't swear here.

Morris I mean, we need to sit down and have a serious talk.

Jean Why don't you just get on with your life?

Morris What life? My life's over, my reason for existing has miraculously disappeared!

Jean You analyse everything. I don't know what's got into you. You didn't used to be bothered. Now it takes you a fortnight to cross the road. You're dead a long time, you know.

Morris That's why I need to talk.

Jean Why, what is it that you want?

Morris I want a break.

Jean A break?

A beat

Morris I mean a change.

Jean From what?

Morris From us.

Jean You mean from me?

Morris Well...

Jean You mean from me?

Morris Yes.

Jean I thought we'd sorted all that?

Morris I want to get away.

Jean On your own?
Morris Yes.
Jean Where to?
Morris Dunno.
Jean What for?
Morris For a month.
Jean I mean, why?
Morris Because.
Jean You've never been away by yourself before.
Morris So I want to do it now!
Jean Even as a kid you never went away by yourself.
Morris Well, I'm forty-one.
Jean You'll be lost.
Morris So, I'll be lost then.
Jean You hate being by yourself.
Morris So I'll hate it then.
Jean Where are you going to go?
Morris Europe. Anywhere. I don't know.
Jean How are you going to get there?
Morris Hey?
Jean How are you going to get there?
Morris I haven't decided yet.
Jean Because you're not going to fly, are you?
Morris Not after last time.
Jean And you won't go on a boat, will you, since the Estonia went down?
Morris I'll get something sorted.
Jean And driving's out?
Morris Don't bring that up.
Jean So it's going to be a walking holiday then, is it?
Morris Not necessarily.
Jean Somewhere flat because of your chest?
Morris I dunno yet.
Jean What are you going to do? Beam yourself into Central Europe.
Morris Maybe.

A beat

Jean And what shall I do?
Morris Count your interest, that's what you do most of the time, isn't it?

A beat

Jean Is this about kids?
Morris No.
Jean What do you want me to do?
Morris Nothing.
Jean There is nothing I can do.
Morris Look, I need a break, that's all. I need to sort things out. This is
    not about you, it's about me. For a change!
Jean For a change?
Morris Yes!
Jean For a change?
Morris Yes!
Jean Don't shout here!
Morris Why are you making this your problem?
Jean For a change?
Morris Hey, this is my mother they've buried here. These are my feelings.
    Do you think I feel nothing? I can't believe you, you have to have a go
    at me on a day like today, don't you?
Jean Oh yeh, that's right.
Morris All this is with you.
Jean Don't blame me.
Morris Bloody lottery!
Jean You should have moved her when I told you.
Morris Don't bring that up!
Jean You should have...
Morris I don't believe this.
Jean She'd've been all right.
Morris Do you think I don't know that!
Jean She would have been happier somewhere else but you didn't want
    to spend the cash. After all you said.
Morris All right, I've heard you.
Jean I told you it was only top clean.
Morris That's right, you've never been wrong in your life, have you?
Jean I was wrong twenty-two years ago...
Morris And so was I?

A young Vicar appears. He has been looking for them

Vicar Ah, here you are...

Morris Hello there!

Vicar I wondered where you'd got to.

Morris Just er...

Vicar I understand.

Jean ...Sharing a few thoughts.

Vicar Yes, of course. You want a quiet moment to yourselves.

Jean If only.

Morris It's...

Vicar A very difficult time I suspect...

Jean It always has been.

Vicar Only time will heal I'm afraid.

Morris Well, that hasn't been our experience, has it?

Jean You can say that again.

Vicar Well, we only have one mother.

Morris In most cases.

Vicar Oh yes.

Morris I'd better go and sort out our Vera. My sister. Her husband only has limited time.

Vicar Is she the lady with the haircut?

Morris You could say that... (*He makes to depart*) I'll just ... thanks very much. I'll just go and see to our Vera, before Doug goes back to prison.

Morris exits

Jean and the Vicar stand in silence

Vicar He seems to be taking it well.

Jean It's afterwards, isn't it?

Vicar Only time, I'm afraid.

Jean Anyway, it was a nice service.

Vicar Thank you.

Jean I haven't seen you before?

Vicar No, that's right. I'm stipendary. I, er, step in when required. I work for Dale Farm full-time, just to erm...

Jean Pay the rent.

Vicar Exactly.

Jean Not a lot of money in it then?

The Vicar ignores this

Vicar You must have been very close?

Jean Only on paper.

Vicar And she was quite a supporter of the church, wasn't she?

Jean Was she?

Vicar So the Rector tells me. I mean, before she was taken ill. Quite a supporter.

Jean I didn't...

Vicar In fact, I'm actually quite pleased to meet you really. Not under these circumstances of course.

Jean Oh yes?

Vicar Yes, I'm quite erm...

Jean Really.

Vicar It's lovely to meet local celebrities.

Jean I didn't know I had so many friends.

Vicar Yes, I'm sure.

Jean They're crawling out from everywhere.

Vicar I bet they are.

Jean You'd be surprised.

Vicar And relatives?

Jean Oh yes!

Vicar Families can be such joy, can't they?

Jean They can be, can't they.

Vicar You know, I shouldn't really tell you this but we have a little flutter ourselves, you know?

Jean You don't?

Vicar Yes, we have the odd flutter.

Jean Oh well?

Vicar In fact, I look forward to Saturdays now. I'm quite a Cilla fan now. I mean it's just a pound a week on the Lottery, the organist and me. We don't tell anyone.

Jean No, I bet you don't!

Vicar But I had to tell you.

Jean Have you won any... ?

Vicar No no ... we had two numbers three weeks and all the others were out by one!

Jean Thank God!

Vicar Absolutely. I don't know what we'd do if we did.

Jean Well, I'd better...

Vicar Yes, must let you go.

Jean Well, thanks again.

Vicar I just wondered if you have any numbers which you could…

Jean Well, I always have my birthday, if that's any help, and our Sarah's, but the rest of 'em I just make up.

Vicar You just make up…?

Jean But I've got a very good feeling about six and forty-two this week.

Vicar Six and forty-two eh? Great, well, thank you very much.

Music

Black-out

SCENE 2

Amsterdam. Tulip field. Day

The tulips of the graveyard now serve as the tulips of Holland

Connie Wilde enters. We see her to be a lithe and attractive woman in her late thirties. She is wheeling a bike on to the stage. She parks the bike, and takes a bag with some Evian water from it. During the following exchange, she will spread out a large table-cloth

Morris enters. He is out of breath

Connie Come on!

Morris I'll tell you sommat, Connie, you're too much for me.

Connie Where've you been?

Morris Where've I been? Didn't you see me? A tractor pulled out, I was up the hedge and nearly in the bloody dyke. I haven't been on a bike since I was seven. Now I know why.

Connie Toughen you up a bit.

Morris You were pedalling on; I could've drowned.

Connie I'd've saved you!

Morris Ten miles on a bike. I think the Tour de France has had it. I bet I can't sit down tomorrow.

Connie You'll have to soak.

Morris You'll have to help me.

Connie I will do.

Morris parks up his bike and surveys the location

Morris I was just looking how flat it is.
Connie Well, Holland is.
Morris Yeh, but this is very flat. This is pancake flat. This is Barbara Lucas flat.
Connie Don't remind me.

Morris joins Connie on the large table-cloth. She proceeds to pass a sandwich and coffee

Morris I haven't had this much exercise in a long time. And I don't mean the bike rides.
Connie Hey, cheeky!
Morris What do you think to the hotel?
Connie Brilliant. But we didn't need a suite, did we? That's just you showing off. Mind you, I never thought I'd stay at the Holiday Inn.
Morris Oh ay, we can stay a month if we want. Mind you, it's bloody expensive.
Connie What about work?
Morris About what? (*He laughs*) Forget it.
Connie Forget it?
Morris Forget it.
Connie Oh yeh?
Morris Forget the clubs. It's just me and you.
Connie Is it?

A beat

Morris It could be.
Connie You've saved me, haven't you?
Morris Yeh.
Connie After twenty-two years?
Morris It's not that long.
Connie It's probably longer.
Morris Get away!
Connie It is. I fancied you right from school.

Morris Get off, nobody fancied me at school.

Connie It's true.

Morris No, I was the kid with the acne.

Connie You weren't that bad.

Morris What, my face looked like a pizza.

Connie What about me?

Morris You looked great.

Connie I looked like a pipe-cleaner, with glasses.

Morris I liked that look. Very sexy.

Connie We were supposed to have a date, can you remember?

Morris When?

Connie But you missed the bus.

Morris I miss everything.

Connie It was a Northern Soul night!

Morris Yeh, I used to do back drops and the splits, bloody hell! How I'll never know.

Connie They had this DJ who was supposed to be from Wigan Casino. Then Angela Smeaton saw him working at Jordan's Butchers, the next morning. What a let down, eh? I spent the whole of that night dancing myself into a frazzle thinking we were in the presence of some great DJ. And there he is the next morning wrapping up half a pound of Cumberland sausage for my Aunty Val.

Morris My mother wouldn't let me go out that night until it had stopped snowing.

Connie I waited but then I went off with Pudding Eastwood!

Morris Pudding Eastwood!!

Connie Pudding Eastwood. He used to smell of Fray Bentos.

Morris He had two heads, didn't he?

Connie He might have had, he had four arms. He was all over me. We went for a snog and a Woodbine; not in that order unfortunately. Then we stood in a bus stop for an hour while he tried to get my bra of!!

Morris Pudding Eastwood...

Connie He was all fingers and thumbs. Finally, I thought sod it, and I took it off myself.

Morris Pudding Eastwood.

Connie Then I just gave it to him and went home. You should've seen his face. He didn't know what to do with it.

Morris That's the night I first saw Jean.

Connie You're joking?

Morris It was at Lifebuoys Disco?

Connie That's it.

Morris Then we arranged to meet again. I don't know why, I hardly knew you.

Connie And I stood you up that time. Just for spite.

Morris I was waiting for you when Jean knocked a Coke down my shirt. She was with Pete Stanley, and trying to shake him off. He used to love Polo mints. Can you remember? He'd get through a couple of packets in a night. He had this perpetual sucking action. This long neck and all.

Connie Yeh, he looked like a skull on a stick.

Morris They married just after that.

Connie Weird, isn't it?

Morris Their bloody marriage was.

Connie What happened to him?

Morris He left her to seek his fortune, went to London.

Connie He missed out there then.

Morris He did and all, he was hit by a bus in Marble Arch. Poor old Pete, if he'd've stuck with Jean he could have been sucking Polo mints every second of the day for the rest of his life!

Connie *(wondering)* All that time...?

Morris Oh yes, I was a wallflower that night.

Connie Poor you.

Morris Sixteen and a loner. I knew then I would end up as a drummer.

Connie Twenty-four years ago.

Morris That's a hell of a lot of *Stand By Your Man*'s.

Connie Too many.

A beat

Morris It was my mother's fault. If it wasn't sunny I had to stay in. There's no wonder I ended up working in security.

Connie Oh well, "All is for the best".

Morris Is it?

Connie Voltaire.

Morris College girl.

Connie For what good it did me.

Morris You've done well.

Connie Not as well as you though.

Morris What about all them lecturers running after you?

Connie Not as many as you think.
Morris I don't want to know.
Connie Yeh, you couldn't move for corduroy jackets.
Morris I know about Kenny anyway.
Connie How come?
Morris I knew about that ages ago. Gordon told me.
Connie Kenny was a mistake.
Morris It was on your birthday. Newcastle.
Connie Twenty-sixth of April. I was thirty-five, alone, depressed, hopelessly drunk, and if you squinted Kenny looked a bit like Kris Kristofferson.
Morris Yeh, but you'd got to really squint though.
Connie Yes, you had.
Morris I mean really squint.
Connie Almost close your eyes.
Morris Yeh, he must have looked like anybody then?
Connie D'you want my cherry?
Morris Steady.
Connie You!
Morris What?
Connie Here!

Connie feeds Morris with a cherry. It is quite sensual. He makes a big play of receiving it

Morris Mmm, feed me.
Connie Like your mother?
Morris I hope not.
Connie Why's that?
Morris I never did the things we've done to my mother.
Connie What about Jean?
Morris No, I don't think Jean did it to my mother either. In fact if anything I think it was the other way round.

A beat

Connie What're you going to do?
Morris Don't spoil it.
Connie She doesn't know, does she? About you being here?

Morris Not with you.
Connie How serious is this?
Morris Serious.
Connie Is it though?
Morris I can't go back…
Connie But she's won the Lottery, three times now!
Morris Exactly!!!
Connie You've always been a bit bloody barmy, haven't you?
Morris But now I can afford to be. Have you any idea how much I'm worth?
Connie You were complaining about the price of the hotel?
Morris Hundred and eighty quid a night! Bloody rip off!!
Connie You bloody tight-arsed gett!
Morris Sore arse, actually.
Connie Oh yeh, I forgot.

Silence

Morris You know that I married the wrong woman, you know that, don't you?
Connie Don't say that.
Morris I did though.
Connie You had Sarah, didn't you?
Morris Uh, talk about feeling bad!
Connie Let's not talk.
Morris Suits me.

Silence. They lie back and listen

Connie Listen. Quiet, isn't it?
Morris This is what we want.
Connie Maybe we're dead.
Morris Well, it suits me.
Connie Do you feel dead?
Morris I feel dead tired.
Connie (*sexily*) Do you know what I'd like to do?
Morris What?
Connie I'd like to tie you up.
Morris What?

Connie Yeh.

Morris Eh?

Connie Yeh.

Morris What for?

Connie Tie you up and rub peanut butter all over you.

Morris What do you think I am?

Connie I've never done that. Have you?

Morris Not recently.

Connie Shall we?

Morris Hey, I know we're in Amsterdam but you don't have to be weird, you know?

Connie Don't you fancy it?

Morris You're going to need a lot of peanut butter, aren't you?

Connie Or we can get some of that Nutella, it spreads easier. I like that.

Morris No way. I draw the line at peanut butter.

Connie Don't you fancy it?

Morris I dunno. Me and Jean usually read a book or do a crossword.

Connie It'll be different then.

Morris I fancy the peanut butter bit but I don't know about the other.

Connie We'll just have that then. Come on, let's go back to the hotel.

Morris Oh, I'm knackered.

Connie Yeh.

Morris What about the bikes?

Connie Leave 'em, we'll hire a car. There's a garage in the village. In fact, we could buy one.

Morris Just to go back?

Connie Well, we could, couldn't we?

Morris Let's buy one then.

Connie Are you serious?

Morris Course I am.

Connie Are you?

Morris Absolutely.

Connie Oh, brilliant.

Morris I haven't felt like this for years.

Connie It's the peanut butter isn't it?

Morris Yeh, I like the nutty bits.

Connie I thought you were nervous about living?

Morris This is not living, is it?

Connie Isn't it?

Morris This is heaven.
Connie You're so full of shit, aren't you?
Morris Yeh, but it's good shit, isn't it?
Connie Yeh, yeh, it's very good shit.

The two of them get off the floor and grab the bikes

Morris Grab a bike and I'll race you to the village.
Connie I thought you were saddle sore?
Morris I am, that's why I want to get a car!
Connie What sort of car do you want?
Morris A blue one.

Connie laughs and follows him off

Music

Black-out

SCENE 3

Jean's new garden. Months later

Jean enters wearing a pair of gardening gloves. She is clearly much more well turned out than we have seen her before. She attends the tulips (which have remained on stage from the previous scene). She has some potting compost with her

Norman, who is still quite unkempt, brings on a small barrow and his swimming gear

Norman Looks good.
Jean Sorry?
Norman Coming on.
Jean Lovely, aren't they?
Norman I didn't know you had green fingers.

Jean shows her pink gloves

Jean I've got pink fingers today.

Norman It's so peaceful sat here.

Jean I've always liked gardening. It was Morris who hated it. He thought all you had to do was to cut the grass.

Norman It's lovely.

Jean Well, it's different.

Norman Different? It's out of this world.

Jean Five hundred thousand.

Norman Gooor.

Jean Yeh.

Norman Worth every penny and all.

Jean It makes Linden Avenue look a bit sad.

Norman It makes our place look a bit sad. It makes me feel like we're living in a rucksack.

Jean I was going to have a toilet put under the stairs but Morris said only Toulouse-Lautrec could use it. So I thought we'd look for somewhere else. I mean, we'd done all we could at Linden. He chose this really.

Norman Well, you had to move, didn't you?

Jean I didn't want to but...

Norman Oh no, you had to. It would've been ridiculous staying where you were. I mean next door were on the dole, weren't they? I mean, talk about coming around for a cup of sugar, they'd've been coming round for a refinery.

Jean Do you like the pool?

Norman Oh ay. I was careful though, I didn't want to splash anything. It looks too nice.

Jean I sometimes go down and look at it, I still can't believe it.

Norman Who lives next door then?

Jean Mr Weatherhill.

Norman The vicar?

Jean He won nine hundred thousand.

Norman Lucky bastard! I'm still trying every week and I haven't won a bean. Look at you, you've won four times!

Jean Yeh, he packed it all in. I think he still does the odd funeral, likes to keep his hand in. (*She is pottering around the garden*)

Norman Don't you have a gardener?

Jean Well I do, but I don't like telling him what to do. So I do most of it myself!

Norman begins to drift around the garden

Norman Must get a bit lonely though?

Jean Well, I'm hardly ever here, am I?

Norman No, I suppose…

Jean I've only been back from Barbados a month.

Norman Is it nice?

Jean Oh, it's warm.

Norman I bet it is.

Jean Oh, it's warm.

Norman Where'd you stay?

Jean Sandy Lane. Oh, it's nice, but it was bloody warm.

Norman Barbados!

Jean You meet some funny buggers though, honestly.

Norman Well, all that lot are up there, aren't they? Bloody bankers, and film stars. They're up there, aren't they, on another planet.

Jean Funny buggers some of 'em.

Norman It's different oxygen, isn't it?

Jean It's different sommat.

Norman I bet they wondered what you did?

Jean I didn't say owt.

Norman Best not to.

Jean I didn't say owt. There was this one bloke from Cheltenham, told me he was worth a million, I thought, ay ay, look out, and I had my ring on. He'd made his money selling socks or sommat.

Norman He must have sold a bloody lot then, because I only pay a quid for mine.

Jean He says, I'm worth a million, you know? He's got this big cigar, bloody gold all over. I thought, yes I am and all, but you can keep your bloody distance, mate! They're all after the same thing.

Norman Mind you, I'd've told him. "A million? Is that all? I spent a million this morning in Asda."

Jean Hey, I met Lauren Bacall, did I tell you?

Norman Did she talk?

Jean Oh yeh, she's ever so nice.

Norman Bloody hell.

Jean Oh, we had a right cal! I didn't ask her about Humphrey Bogart, you know I thought I'd keep off personal stuff. Oh ay, we had a right chat!

A beat, as Jean finishes her gardening

Norman How do you think she'll do?

Jean I think she'll be all right.

Norman Do you?

Jean Well, I know the consultant, he said she should be OK. I gave 'em two hundred thousand for research last month. I mean, they've got no cash down there!

Norman She's a funny bugger is your Annie but I mean, she's never smoked, has she?

Jean I know.

Norman Never smoked.

Jean Mind you, my mam had it you know?

Norman Ay, she said.

Jean She'll be all right. They're just keeping her in for tests, aren't they?

Norman I'll feel a lot better when she comes out. I didn't realize I'd miss the daft old sod so much.

Jean She'll be all right.

Norman Do you think...?

Morris sheepishly appears. He carries a holdall

Silence, and an icy tension between the three of them

Morris Right then...

Jean Got what you want?

Morris Just about.

Jean How do you get there?

Morris I get the train to Waterloo then I take the Chunnel to Brussels, then another train. It's not so bad.

Norman There's been an accident, hasn't there, in that tunnel?

Morris When?

Norman Yesterday, wasn't it? I think a train caught fire or sommat.

Jean Don't tell him that, rail travel's the only thing he dare go on.

Morris I never heard about that?

Norman It was in the paper.

Morris I didn't see it.

Norman They had to get 'em all off. Smoke everywhere apparently.

Jean Don't tell him that, Norman, he might want to stay.

Morris Yeh, well.

Jean He thinks he's going to drop dead any minute. We don't want him dying on us, do we?

Morris Anyway!

Jean But obviously when he gets to Amsterdam he turns into Superman or somebody.

Norman Ay, well, it's a good trick if you can do it!

Jean Not a care in the world.

Morris Very good.

Jean Yeh, when he's in Holland he thinks he's Peter Pan. It must be the air.

Morris Must be something.

Jean I knew he'd go somewhere flat.

Norman Can you see fish under the Chunnel then?

Morris You what?

Norman Fish, can you see 'em?

Jean He won't be able to tell you, he probably keeps his eyes shut!

Norman I'd got this impression that you'd be able to see bloody fish and all sorts. Be all right that, sat there looking at fish... Aren't they supposed to reduce your blood pressure?

Morris No, it's just black.

Jean The way I feel.

Norman Mind you, we had a goldfish and it didn't reduce my blood pressure. In fact, I nearly had a stroke every day keeping it alive.

A beat

Jean So, this is it then?

Morris Yeh.

Jean You're not coming back?

Morris No.

Jean Right.

Morris Yeh.

Jean What shall I do with the car then? I kept it for you.

Morris What, as a reminder?

Norman I'll have it if you don't want it.

Morris Give it to Norman.

Norman I've always liked that car...

Morris Beats a soap-on-a-rope eh?

Jean What about your stuff?

Morris I've got what I want.

Jean (*referring to his small holdall*) Just that?

Morris This and my bank stuff.

Jean He thinks he's Dick Whittington don't you?

Morris I've got what I need.

Jean So I'll burn the rest of 'em, shall I?

Morris If you want.

Jean Right, I'll burn 'em then.

Morris Right. Well, all the best, mate. I hope Annie's…

Norman Yeh yeh, right.

Morris I'm sure she will be.

Norman Fingers crossed anyway.

Jean I'll make sure she's looked after.

Morris She'll be fine. She's a fighter your Annie, isn't she?

Norman Oh ay.

Morris Yeh.

Norman Oh ay, she's a fighter.

Morris Right then.(*He turns to go*)

Jean You know you're getting off light, aren't you?

Morris Am I?

Jean I won, not you.

Morris What's up, haven't you got enough? I'm surprised you're out here doing the garden, I thought you might be doing another lottery or filling the pools in or sommat?

Jean Well, you've never been lucky, have you?

Morris I was lucky in love, Jean.

Jean Were you?

Morris Yeh, lucky in love.

A beat

Jean How will I get in touch then?

Morris You won't. This is what I'm saying.

Jean Right then.

Morris I should've done it years ago.

Jean Should you?

Morris It's nowt to do with you.

Jean That's right, it's nowt to do with me, is it?

Morris Anyway!

A beat

Jean Is she happy then?
Morris Yeh. She is actually.
Jean Finally got what she wanted.
Morris No, I got what I wanted.
Jean Waken up.
Morris I have done.
Jean You're softer than I thought.
Morris No, I'm not.
Jean It all becomes the same thing. Believe me.
Morris What film are you in now?
Jean *Gone With the Wind.* What are you in, *Love Story*?
Morris That's right. (*He makes a move to go. He picks up the holdall*)
Jean Be careful when you're crossing the road, you know! I wouldn't want anything to happen to you.
Morris No, that's right!

Morris exits

Silence. Jean is very distraught. Norman doesn't know what to say

Norman Shall I give you a hand with them tulips, Jean, or what? I'll get some more compost, shall I, and give you a bit of a hand?
Jean No, leave it.
Norman It's no problem.
Jean Just...
Norman Right. I'll leave it then, shall I?

Silence

Jean That bloody man. (*She is quite upset*)

Norman is embarrassed by the emotion

Norman I didn't think he'd go to be honest. I mean, he's always been full of hot air, hasn't he? He's always been going to do this that and the other? Look at his drumming. I mean, he thought he was Cosy Powell, didn't he, and he didn't have any rhythm. I went to see 'em in Doncaster once. She could sing. I mean there's no denying that. She's a good singer. But you see what she was. She could sing though, credit where

it's due, and the rest of the band were all right, a bit Chickory Tip, but
Morris was all over the shop. I was talking to her at the bar. I mean, I'm
going back six years, maybe more. She said they'd been trying to get rid
of him for ages but they didn't know anybody who had their own drum
kit.

Jean is very upset

Hey, are you all right?

Jean Yeh, I'm fan-bloody-tastic!

Norman Do you want to go for a swim or...?

Jean All this time, eh?

Norman Shall we go and sit in the sauna...?

Jean All this time I've been kidding myself. Telling myself that he
wouldn't go. I must be bloody barmy.

Norman Shall we have a game of croquet or sommat...?

Jean That bloody man.

Norman Well, I don't know what to say.

Jean That bloody man!

Norman Shall I get packed up? I'll sort the barrow out, shall I?

Jean I love him, you know.

Norman Hey, come on.

Jean I love him ... though...

Norman I know.

Jean is sobbing heavily

Jean For all he's done I still bloody love him. I must be three sheets to the
wind.

The Lights fade on Jean and Norman

Jean and Norman exit

Black-out

SCENE 4

Amsterdam. Night. Weeks later

Connie enters. She is dressed up for a night on the town. She has clearly been for a meal. She carries a bottle of champagne and a glass

Morris enters. He is dressed in a white tuxedo. He is slightly worse for drink

They are looking at the canals of Amsterdam. We should get the impression that they are on a bridge near a canal

Connie Here he is.
Morris Here I am.
Connie Peanut man.
Morris James Bond.
Connie James Bond?
Morris Hello, Miss Moneypenny.
Connie Hello, Mr Peanut.
Morris Hey hey listen, who's that actress who played Pussy Galore?
Connie Honor Blackman?
Morris No, on a motor bike actually.
Connie What?
Morris It's a joke.
Connie How is it?
Morris Because it's funny.
Connie I don't get it.
Morris Wait till later.
Connie You're all talk.
Morris What?
Connie Nothing.
Morris This is like a blind date, isn't it?
Connie How is it?
Morris Well, we're both blind drunk, aren't we?
Connie You are.
Morris I've got that much plastic on me, if I stood by a fire I'd melt. There'd be plastic running down my trouser legs.
Connie And that's not all.

Morris Hang on, hang on.

Silence. Morris clicks his fingers twice

Connie What's that?
Morris I've just earned another three hundred quid. (*He laughs*)
Connie Hang on. (*She clicks her fingers*) I've just spent it.

Both laugh uproariously

Morris Here, have a credit card. (*He gives Connie one of his credit cards*)
Connie What is this?
Morris It's a gift.
Connie It's got my name on it.
Morris Spend what you want.
Connie You've got more cards than Paul Daniels.
Morris I've got more money than sense.
Connie You have and all.
Morris No wonder I've got a limp. I bet my wallet alone weighs two
   stone.

A beat

   I paid all that and didn't have a clue what I was eating.
Connie Veal brains.
Morris Was that it?
Connie That's what I had.
Morris I've never had so many courses. They don't feed you up so much,
   as bore you to death. And you know why it's so expensive, don't you?
Connie Because it's select. They don't let just anybody in.
Morris It's with all them hangers on floating about.
Connie Oh, I like that.
Morris They're hovering about like vultures. Soon as you've finished,
   woooof your plate's gone and the next thing you know there's some sad
   twat sweeping your table, with a silver dustpan. That alone costs you
   thirty quid!!
Connie It probably does and all!
Morris And if you can actually see the food on your plate it's a bloody
   miracle. But there it is, about as big as a gnat's bollock, but they call it

food. And the sweets are about as big as sommat you could stick up your arse, and to be honest mine looked like that's where it came from. And finally the top lad sneaks up to you with his shit breath and asks, "Has everything been all right?" Like he's not sure. How do I know? I didn't even know what I'd bloody ordered.

Connie How much was it?

Morris Bloody hell, all that money to be pampered. I used to be satisfied with fish and chips, and a spring roll.

Connie Easily satisfied, aren't you, Morris?

Morris I am and all.

Connie More suited to the simple life, aren't you?

Morris No, this is the stuff. Look at that watch, guess how much? Eight hundred quid. Shoes, Peter Lord thirty-nine ninety-five, this jacket cost a bloody fortune.

Connie But you'd rather have fish and chips?

Morris I would.

Connie Get away.

Morris Fish and chips in the paper, a carton of mushy peas.

Connie A pie?

Morris Ay, a pie and all.

Connie And some scraps.

Morris Oh yes!

Connie All mixed together in the paper, and you sat on the seafront at Hornsea. Freezing to bloody death.

Morris Hey?

Connie And then you think what shall we do next? Shall we walk to that shelter for five minutes or shall we walk to that other shelter? Oh, shall we have another game of bingo. Another? We've already had six million games today, and all we've won is a bottle of jam.

Morris Hey, listen!

Connie You don't want to go back to that, do you?

Morris Hey, don't knock it.

Connie "What shall we do tomorrow then?" Walk and have a game of bingo and then we can go and decide which shelter we're going to sit in before it snows and we both get pneumonia.

Morris I'll tell you this, it beats paying six hundred quid for a bloody meal you can't even see.

Connie So you'd want to go back then?

Morris Talk sense!

Connie So don't keep going on about it.
Morris But they must be pinching money.
Connie Oh, don't start all that.
Morris All what?
Connie You know what!
Morris What?
Connie You know what!
Morris Don't tell me what to do.
Connie Well, don't go on then.
Morris Don't tell me what to do.
Connie Why not?
Morris Because you're offside!
Connie And is there anything else you don't like?
Morris Just don't tell me what to do!
Connie (*mocking*) Don't tell me what to do!
Morris I don't like it.
Connie I don't like you snoring all night, but I don't say anything.
Morris What are you saying?
Connie It's like being in bed with a bloody animal. I don't know how she put up with you.
Morris She had a strong stomach.
Connie I bet she did.
Morris And she was a deep sleeper.
Connie She must have been a bloody saint.
Morris Oh, you're well offside!
Connie You never stop do you, on and on and on…
Morris You never stop either, do you?
Connie On and on, you're like an old chicken, clucking away.
Morris It's you, you talk such rubbish.
Connie She must have turned off most of the time. Come to think of it, she wouldn't ever be turned on, would she?
Morris Offside!
Connie Do me a favour, Morris, I've seen more rhythm in a stick!
Morris Oh, we've had a few drinks, have we?
Connie You couldn't keep a beat at the best of times, so how you and Jean ever managed to do anything is beyond me. I mean we were trying to ditch you for two years. You kept putting these extra drum rolls in, Kenny thought you'd got a twitch. Why did you leave her, she was everything you needed, wasn't she? Somebody to mother you.

Morris I left a woman with twenty million for this?

Connie You don't wear it well, Morris, do you?

Morris This feels… I tell you this, I've been here before, love.

Connie "Well since my mother died!"

Morris Don't you drag that up.

Connie "Since we lost our Sarah."

Morris Offside.

Connie It wasn't your fault she died, it was an accident. But you just walked away, didn't you? The car was a right-off, but you got out without a scratch. That's what luck is, Morris, I call that bloody lucky!

Morris I've been here before, old love.

Connie What are you like? "Every day I think my luck'll run out, every day I think my heart's going to stop, I live every day as my last because one day I know I'm going to be right."

Morris Well, I do.

Connie We all do.

Morris Are we arguing?

Connie Come on, let's get some money spent!

Morris How?

Connie Casino.

Morris No … throwing money away!! Where is it?

Connie The ring road.

Morris We can get a cab. We can buy a cab!

Connie Take the car.

Morris What, at this time?

Connie Come on, live a bit…

Morris is fired by Connie's bravado. He moves closer to her, he holds her in a clinch

Morris Ohh.

Connie Yeh.

Morris You're evil.

Connie I know.

Morris You're spending all my money, aren't you?

Connie But there's so much of it to spend, isn't there.

Morris Oh, I love it when you say that!

Connie Yeh?

Morris Give us a kiss then!

Connie kisses Morris

Connie How's that?
Morris Thank you and good night! Taxi!

Connie and Morris exit

Music

Black-out

SCENE 5

Jean's home. Three days later. Bird-song

Norman enters. He puts a small box over the flowers, and then takes from the barrow a large winter protection sheet and places it over the garden bench. He has a cold, he stops and blows his nose

Morris enters. He has his belongings with him, including a small suitcase

Morris All right then?
Norman All right.
Morris Stranger in Paradise eh?
Norman I wondered who it was.
Morris She's got you a new job then?
Norman Just getting ready for winter. It's going to be a bad 'un according to Mr Fish.
Morris Smashing, just what we want eh?

A beat

Norman Back then?
Morris Uuphh! Eh… Bloody hell!
Norman Yeh?
Morris I wouldn't advise it.
Norman No?
Morris Twenty-two years.

Norman That's right.

Morris We make some bloody mistakes.

Norman We do.

Morris Well, I do. It was costing me a fortune in peanut butter.

Norman In what?

Morris She was driving me round the bend. Hey, I even flew back, that's how much I missed Jean, eh.

Norman A bit desperate then?

Morris Not much. Oh, Norman, we make some bloomers, don't we? I was that desperate to get back I bought a hire car.

Norman You should see that one of mine now. I've got trims on it and all sorts. Take the kids all over in it.

Morris Good.

Norman Thanks for that.

Morris How's Annie?

Norman Not wonderful to be honest. She's to have some more tests. I mean, she's still weak, and they don't know if they've caught the whatsit?

Morris Oh dear!

Norman But she's a fighter is Annie.

A beat

Morris Ay, I saw you down here, I thought you were breaking in.

Norman There's been some. Vicar's been broken into three times. Mind you, you'd have to be in the bloody SAS to break into "Jeamo". Jean had it all wired up.

Morris Probably to stop me coming back.

Norman No...

Morris You never know.

Norman Well?

Morris You know me and Jean...

Norman That's right...

A beat

Morris Where is she?

Norman Eh?

Morris Where is she?

Norman We didn't know how to get in touch with you, Morris.

Morris No, I know...

Norman Otherwise...

Morris What's...

Norman I dunno...

Morris What're you on about?

Norman Eh, Morris... I'm ever so sorry.

Morris What's up, what's happened?

Norman We couldn't tell you.

Morris Where is she?

Norman There's been an accident...

Morris Fucking hell...

Norman I know...

Morris Oh fuck...

Norman Morris, mate...

Morris Oh dear ... this is just ... fucking hell ... I mean...

Norman I know.

Morris Is she?

Norman I don't want to be the one, mate...

Morris Oh no...

Norman We couldn't get in touch...

Morris When?

Norman Last week.

Morris What happened?

Norman She was just crossing the road from the video shop, when somebody hit her.

Morris Bloody hell...

Norman They reckon she wouldn't have known much about it.

Morris Oh God.

Norman I didn't know what video she'd got or owt like that. I mean, I don't know any of the detail. She was taking *Deathwish* back, because we watched it with her. She was happy as a sandman. And then just, bang ... bloody hell. Poor Jean.

Morris Bloody hell.

Norman Funny thing is, Moss, she told me she had a good feeling about tonight's lottery. Goor eh? And you know she was giving it all away? She gave the hospital a million, and the Scouts. Apparently they came to do "bob a job" and Jean gave 'em a cheque for three hundred thousand.

Morris Bloody hell.
Norman We've still not seen a penny though.
Morris Bloody hell...
Norman Funeral's tomorrow.
Morris Oh Jean...
Norman I was just... She loved this garden.
Morris Oh Jeanie...
Norman She missed you.
Morris Oh hell.
Norman Ay, she really missed you, mate.

Annie enters, she is clearly unwell, but at this time she appears to be somewhat elated. She is shocked and surprised to see Morris

.
You all right?
Annie Stop fussing with me.
Norman I just want to make sure she's all right.
Annie I am now!
Norman Ay, Morris's back!
Annie Oh Morris...
Morris (*still upset*) I know...
Annie Oh eh?
Morris I know.
Annie I can't believe it after all this time.
Morris Don't go upsetting yourself, love.
Annie I don't know what to say.
Morris There's nowt you can say, is there?
Annie I mean, I never thought...
Morris I know, Annie, I should never have gone.
Annie I still can't believe it.
Morris A bloody week too late.
Norman He's back now though.
Morris Oh eh?
Annie I mean, I thought I was only going to get two, but I ended up getting five.
Morris Eh?
Norman You what?
Annie Yeh, I know...
Norman Five what?

Annie Five and the bonus ball.

Norman You what?

Annie I can't believe it.

Norman Oh what?

Annie And there's twenty million to share this week.

Morris Eh?

Annie I've just rang up. They reckon we should be in with eighty thousand.

Norman Oh God...

Annie I know...

Norman Oh hell.

Morris Oh eh.

Norman Oh shit.

Morris Orrrghhh...

Norman Oh sorry, mate, but, I mean I can't stop smiling. Oh this is awful, sorry, Morris mate, look at me grinning.

Morris Oh Jean.

Annie I can't believe it. I'm shakin' all over, I could dance I could, but my legs are like water. I was just sat there then up they came. I mean, I was going to follow Jean's numbers, but I went with my own. And look at this, Jean didn't even get a number this week... Here look...

Annie offers Jean's ticket to Morris

Morris Oh shit.

Norman Sorry about smiling mate!

Morris Oh eh?

Annie I'll go back and get the sherry out, shall I? If I can find the key. She hid everything you know... I'm glad you're back. She would have wanted that!

Annie exits

Silence. Morris and Norman are awkward with each other

Morris Oh well.

Norman I could cry, Moss. I've never had so much.

Morris No right.

Norman I mean, I thought it was all a fix. I thought nobody really won.

Except for Jean. Mind you, eighty thousand's nowt compared with you, is it?

Morris That's right.

Norman I mean, it's just loose change, isn't it?

Morris That's right.

Norman I'd better nip and see what Annie's…

Morris Yeh, yeh.

Norman Sorry, Moss, but I just can't stop smiling.

Morris Yeh.

Norman Yeh, well … we're lucky sods, aren't we?

Norman exits

Morris stands alone. He tears up Jean's lottery ticket

Morris That's right, Norman. That's dead right! (*He scatters the lottery ticket*)

Music: Hot Chocolate's You Win Again

The Lights fade to black

CURTAIN

FURNITURE AND PROPERTY LIST

Further dressing may be added at the director's discretion

ACT I

SCENE 1

On stage: Standard lamp
2 chairs
TV
Newspaper
Chest of drawers

SCENE 2

On stage: As before

Off stage: Outdoor coat, security jumper (**Morris**)
Bottle of champagne, some glasses (**Norman**)

SCENE 3

Set: Large hospital bed

SCENE 4

Strike: Large hospital bed

Off stage: Large flowers (**Waiter**)
Expensive shopping bags and boxes (**Jean**)

SCENE 5

On stage: As before

Off stage: Handful of letters (**Annie**)

Personal: **Morris:** paper crown

ACT II

SCENE 1

Set: Red wooden tulips

SCENE 2

Off stage: Bike. *In it:* bag containing Evian water, large table-cloth,
                sandwich, coffee, a cherry (**Connie**)
                Bike (**Morris**)

SCENE 3

On stage: Red wooden tulips
                Garden bench
                Small bag

Off stage: Some potting compost (**Jean**)
                Small barrow, swimming gear (**Norman**)

Personal: **Jean:** gardening gloves

SCENE 4

Off stage: Bottle of champagne, glass (**Connie**)

Personal: **Morris:** credit cards

SCENE 5

Off stage: Small box, barrow containing large winter protection sheet
                (**Norman**)
                His belongings, including a small suitcase (**Morris**)
                Lottery ticket (**Annie**)

Personal: **Norman:** handkerchief

LIGHTING PLOT

Property fittings required: standard lamp
3 interior, 4 exterior settings

ACT I, SCENE 1

To open: House lights on, then fade to black-out

Cue 1   Music quickly fades   (Page 1)
           Bring up lights quickly

Cue 2   **Jean** and **Morris** groan in unison   (Page 1)
           Further fade up lights

Cue 3   Jim Capaldi's *Love Hurts* plays   (Page 5)
           Black-out

ACT I, SCENE 2

To open: Overall general lighting

Cue 4   **Jean**: "Look out it's back!!"   (Page 11)
           Black-out

Cue 5   **All** laugh   (Page 12)
           Slowly bring up lights

Cue 6   Four Seasons' *Storm in a Teacup* plays   (Page 17)
           Black-out

ACT I, SCENE 3

To open: Overall general lighting

Cue 7	Music plays	(Page 21)
	Black-out	

ACT I, SCENE 4

To open:	Overall general lighting	

Cue 8	Music plays	(Page 31)
	Black-out	

ACT I, SCENE 5

To open:	Overall general lighting	

Cue 9	Hot Chocolate's *You Win Again* plays	(Page 40)
	Fade to black-out	

ACT II, SCENE 1

To open:	Dismal drizzling day lighting	

Cue 10	Music plays	(Page 48)
	Black-out	

ACT II, SCENE 2

To open:	Overall general lighting	

Cue 11	Music plays	(Page 55)
	Black-out	

ACT II, SCENE 3

To open:	Overall general lighting	

Cue 12	**Jean**: "I must be three sheets to the wind."	(Page 62)
	Fade lights on **Jean** *and* **Norman**	

Cue 13   **Jean** and **Norman** exit   (Page 62)
             Black-out

ACT II, Scene 4

To open: Night-time lighting

Cue 14   Music plays   (Page 68)
             Black-out

ACT II, Scene 5

To open: Overall general lighting

Cue 15   Hot Chocolate's *You Win Again* plays   (Page 73)
             Fade lights to black

EFFECTS PLOT

ACT I

Cue 1   To open   (Page 1)
Music: Hot Chocolate's It Started with a Kiss,
    then quickly fade

Cue 2   **Jean** watches TV   (Page 5)
Music: Jim Capaldi's Love Hurts

Cue 3   **Jean** watches *Blind Date*   (Page 6)
Fade music

Cue 4   **Morris** and **Norman** laugh   (Page 17)
Music: Four Seasons' Storm in a Teacup

Cue 5   **Molly**: "…you're a bloody mess!!!"   (Page 21)
Music

Cue 6   **Morris** and **Jean** exit   (Page 31)
Music

Cue 7   **Jean**: "I've got that!"   (Page 40)
Music: Hot Chocolate's You Win Again

ACT II

Cue 8   To open   (Page 41)
Music: Sweet Sensation's Sad Sweet Dreamer

Cue 9   **Vicar**: "Great, well, thank you very much."   (Page 48)
Music

Cue 10   **Connie** exits   (Page 55)
Music

Cue 11   **Connie** and **Morris** exit   (Page 68)
Music

Cue 12   To open Scene 5   (Page 68)
              Bird-song

Cue 13   **Morris** scatters the lottery ticket   (Page 73)
              Music: Hot Chocolate's You Win Again

A licence issued by Samuel French Ltd to perform this play does not include permission to use the Incidental music specified in this copy. Where the place of performance is already licensed by the PERFORMING RIGHT SOCIETY a return of the music used must be made to them. If the place of performance is not so licensed then application should be made to the Performing Right Society, 29 Berners Street, London W1.

A separate and additional licence from PHONOGRAPHIC PERFORMANCES LTD, Ganton House, Ganton Street, London W1 is needed whenever commercial recordings are used.